The MAILBOX®

Laura McGuigan

Organize MAY Now!™

Everything You Need for a Successful May

M000267011

Monthly Organizing Tools
Manage your time, classroom, and students with monthly organizational tools.

Thematic Idea Collections
Practice essential skills this month with engaging activities and reproducibles.

May in the Classroom
Carry your monthly themes into every corner of the classroom.

Ready-to-Go Learning Centers and Skills Practice
Bring May to life right now!

Managing Editor: Allison E. Ward

Editorial Team: Becky S. Andrews, Kimberley Bruck, Karen P. Shelton, Diane Badden, Thad H. McLaurin, Sharon Murphy, Cindy K. Daoust, Lynn Drolet, Gerri Primak, Karen A. Brudnak, Hope Rodgers, Dorothy C. McKinney, Janet Boyce, Roxanne LaBell Dearman, Deborah Garmon, Ada Goren, Lucia Kemp Henry, Jenny Kerr, Gail Madden, Carrie Maly, Christy McNeal, Suzanne Moore, Keely Peasner, Krystal St. Louis, Susan Walker

Production Team: Lisa K. Pitts, Pam Crane, Rebecca Saunders, Jennifer Tipton Cappoen, Chris Curry, Sarah Foreman, Theresa Lewis Goode, Clint Moore, Greg D. Rieves, Barry Slate, Donna K. Teal, Zane Williard, Tazmen Carlisle, Cat Collins, Marsha Heim, Amy Kirtley-Hill, Lynette Dickerson, Mark Rainey, Angela Kamstra, Debbie Shoffner

www.themailbox.com

Manufactured in the United States
10 9 8 7 6 5 4 3 2

Table of Contents

Monthly Organizing Tools

A collection of reproducible forms, notes, and other timesavers and organizational tools just for May.

Thematic Idea Collections

Fun, child-centered ideas for your favorite May themes.

May in the Classroom

In a hurry to find a specific type of May activity? It's right here!

Ready-to-Go Learning Centers and Skills Practice

Two center activities you can tear out and use today! Plus a collection of May-themed reproducibles for fine-motor skills practice!

Skills Grid

	Strawberries	Flowers	Butterflies	Mother's Day	Centers	Circle Time & Centers	Learning Center: Flower Power	Learning Center: Busy Bees	Ready-to-Go Skills Practice
Literacy									
recognizing letters	18								
prewriting	20		39	46					
mixed practice	21								
rhymes		27							
following directions		28							
beginning sound /d/		35							
beginning sounds			38						
rhyming pictures			45						
print awareness				46					
matching letters in own name					60				
visual discrimination					62				
matching letters						66			
matching uppercase and lowercase letters								82	
Language Development									
participate in song		27							
oral language			36						
following directions						67			
Math									
sorting by color	19								
mixed practice	21								
shapes	24								
matching sets	25				61				
patterns		26							
colors		28							
classification		29							
positional words			37						
spatial sense			38						
comparing size			44						
matching numbers					62				
extending patterns							74		
Science									
sensory exploration	18								
scientific knowledge		26							
life stages			36						
Physical Health & Development									
gross-motor skills	19	29				67			
fine-motor skills	21				60				
tracing									90, 91, 92, 93
cut and paste									94, 95, 96
Creative Arts									
using art media	20		37						
movement			39						
dramatic play					61				
Approaches to Learning									
reasoning						66			

name

is "berry" SPECIAL because...

date

teacher

©The Mailbox® • *Organize May Now!*™ • TEC60973

Contents: Good News!

©The Mailbox® • *Organize May Now!*™ • TEC60973

I'm All Aflutter!

©The Mailbox® • *Organize May Now!*™ • TEC60973

Awards: Use these awards to reinforce positive behaviors.

TEC60973

Headband

Glue to a construction paper strip sized to fit around a child's head.

Wristband

Tape the ends together where shown.

Medallion

Tape to a child's clothing or to a crepe paper necklace.

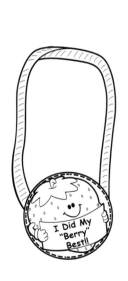

Headband, wristband, and medallion: Copy on colorful construction paper and use as desired.

May

Sunday	Monday	Tuesday	Wednesday	Thursday	Friday	Saturday

©The Mailbox® • *Organize May Now!*™ • TEC60973

Center Checklist

Name	Center								

CLASS LIST

Name											

Classroom News

Date _____

From _____

Help Wanted

Please Remember

Look What We Are Learning

☆ Superstars ☆

Special Thanks

Classroom News

Date _____

From _____

Royal News

Clip art: Use the artwork on student papers and on correspondence such as announcements, forms, and parent notes.

Materials to Collect:

Duties This Month:

Meetings:

To Do:

Birthdays & Special Dates:

Themes:

Monthly planning form: Use this handy form to stay on top of May's school-related responsibilities.

Table and cubby tags: Copy these tags on construction paper and personalize them with your youngsters' names. If desired, laminate the tags for durability.

©The Mailbox® • *Organize May Now!*™ • TEC60973

Open Page: Use this page for parent correspondence and use it with students too. For example, ask a child to draw herself holding a flower bouquet or have her dictate a Mother's Day message to a loved one.

Dear Parent,

Please remember

_____ date

Thanks! You're the "be-zzzz-t"!

Parent reminder note: Use this note to remind parents of supply requests, field trips, and special events such as classroom parties, school programs, or guest speakers.

School Note

©The Mailbox® • *Organize May Now!*™ • TEC60973

SCHOOL NOTE

©The Mailbox® • *Organize May Now!*™ • TEC60973

School notes: Use these notes for parent communications such as announcing an upcoming event, requesting supplies or volunteers, and writing messages of praise.

Let your child's creativity bloom with this special project! Please help your child draw a picture of himself or herself in the center of the flower. Then cut out the flower pattern and have your child decorate the flower petals with a variety of art supplies, such as paint, crayons, or yarn.

We hope to see your project by _____.

Sincerely,

Name _____

Learning Links: develops fine-motor skills

Note to the teacher: Date and sign a copy of the page. Then make student copies on white construction paper. Write a child's name on the flower before sending it home with her. When she returns her project, invite her to share it with her classmates. Then attach a green crepe paper streamer stem and add it to a display titled "Bloomin' With Pride!"

Strawberries

Super Strawberries!

They look	red
	heart shaped
	small
They smell	sweet
	like fruit drink
	yummy
They feel	soft
	bumpy
	squishy
They sound	quiet
	like nothing
They taste	juicy
	delicious
	like candy

"Sense-ational" Strawberries

To prepare for this sweet treat, wash and dry a class supply of whole strawberries. Prepare a chart similar to the one shown but without the responses. Give each child a berry and ask her to look at it. Read aloud the first sentence starter on the chart; then have volunteers dictate as you write to complete it. Continue in this manner for the next three sentence starters. Then, with great fanfare, invite each child to taste her berry and describe the flavor. Complete the chart with student dictation, and then, if desired, provide more fresh, juicy strawberries for a snack.

Strawberries and Caps

Using the patterns on page 22, make a supply of construction paper strawberries and caps. Program a berry and cap with the same letter. Repeat with the remaining strawberries and caps to make a desired number of letter pairs; then place the berries and caps at a center. A child says the letter and then pairs each strawberry with the appropriate cap. For added challenge, program the berries with lowercase letters and program the caps with matching uppercase letters.

This patch of learning is just ripe
for your youngsters!

Sorting by color

Just the Red Ones, Please!

Uh-oh! Somebody picked all the strawberries but didn't know that only the red ones are ripe and ready to eat. Place a pail filled with red, pink, and light green pom-poms (strawberries) at a center. Cut off and discard the tops of three paper lunch bags. Label the bags as shown and then add them to the center. A child in this center sorts the strawberries by color and places them in the appropriate bag.

Physical Health & Development

Gross-motor skills

Strawberry Shake!

Shake up parachute play in a whole new way! Have students grip the edges of a parachute (or sheet) and pull it taut. Toss on ten large red pom-poms to resemble strawberries. Then invite youngsters to shake the parachute until all the berries have flown off. Have volunteers collect the stray strawberries and put them back on the parachute for another round of Strawberry Shake.

Strawberry Foods Forever

What strawberry-flavored foods do your youngsters prefer? Find out with this class book. With students, brainstorm a list of foods that contain strawberries or are strawberry flavored. Next, give each child a white construction paper copy of page 23. As she dictates, write her preferred strawberry food. Invite her to illustrate her page and then paint her strawberry food with red or pink paint that's been scented with strawberry drink mix. When the paint is dry, bind the pages behind a construction paper cover and add a title.

Using art media · · · · · · · · · · · · · · · · · · **Creative Arts**

Very Big Berries

These giant strawberries are just right for little hands! Cut a class supply of large strawberry shapes from red construction paper. Have each child make white fingerprint seeds all over a strawberry. When the paint is dry, invite her to tear a half sheet of green construction paper into several smaller pieces and then glue them to the top to resemble a strawberry cap and stem. Personalize each child's berry to complete the project.

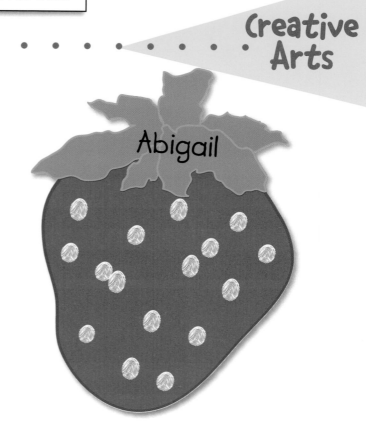

"Berry" Best Bakery

Transform your play dough center into a bakery that specializes in strawberry goodies! Stock the center with a variety of child-safe baking equipment such as cake pans, muffin tins, pie plates, small rolling pins, spatulas, measuring spoons, and cookie cutters. Scent batches of red and pink play dough with strawberry drink mix and store them in airtight containers. If desired, include other colors of play dough, such as tan (crusts and dough), white (whipped topping and ice cream), and green (stems and leaves). Little ones are sure to enjoy whipping up a fresh batch of tasty strawberry creations!

Literacy or Math

Mixed practice

Fresh-Picked Practice

This musical trip to the strawberry patch provides plenty of skill reinforcement! Use the patterns on page 63 to make a class supply of small strawberry cutouts. Program each berry with a letter, number, or shape and then scatter them in an open area. Teach youngsters the song shown and then lead them in singing while they walk around the strawberry patch. At the end of the verse, have each child pick a berry and identify the letter (or number or shape). Then have youngsters return the strawberries to the patch for another round of singing and picking!

(sung to the tune of "The Mulberry Bush")

Here we go through the strawberry patch,
The strawberry patch, the strawberry patch.
Here we go through the strawberry patch.
It's time to pick a berry.

Find additional reproducible activities on pages 24 and 25.

TEC60973

Strawberries are a yummy treat!

Strawberry _____ can't be beat!

Note to the teacher: Use with "Strawberry Foods Forever" on page 20.

Shapes in a Strawberry

Name _____

Color the ☐ s green.
Color the ◯ s red.

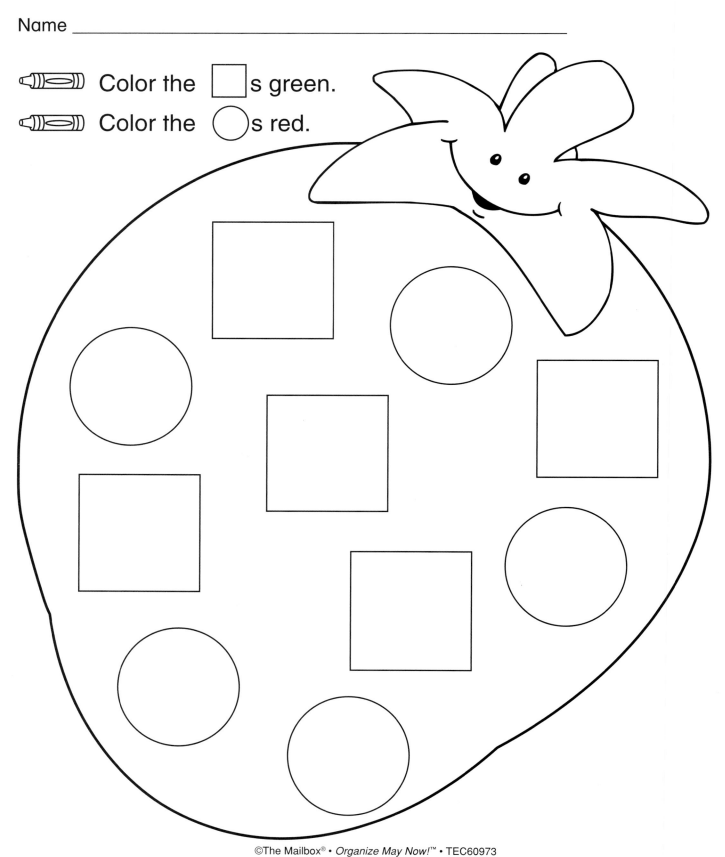

"Berry" Good Sets

Name _____

✂ Cut.

Match.

Glue.

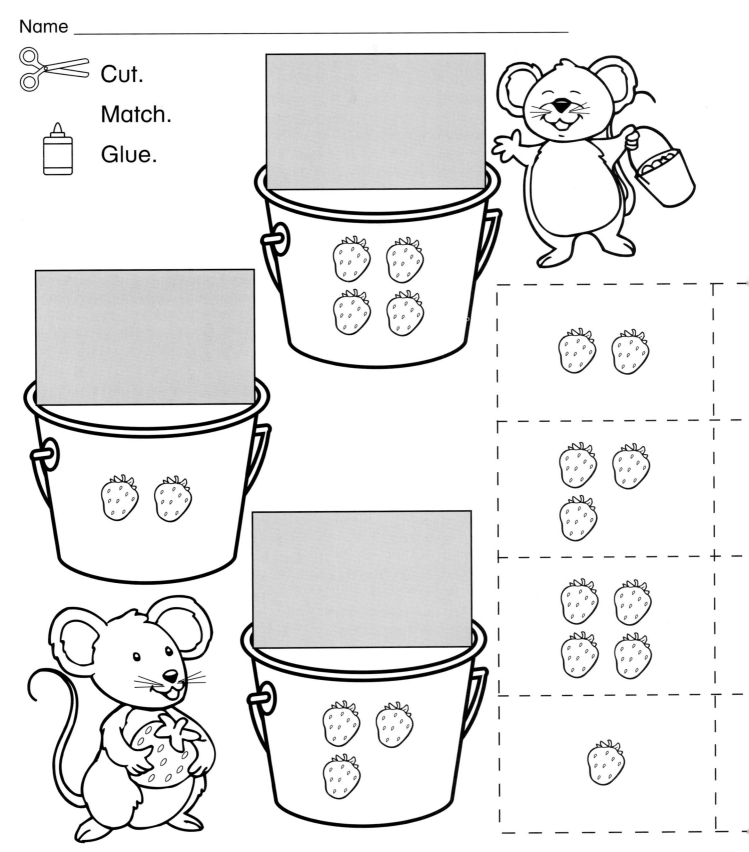

Flowers

From Seed to Flower

The simple text and illustrations in these blooming booklets help little ones understand how a seed grows into a flower. For each student, cut out the booklet cover, booklet pages, and patterns on pages 30–32. Sequence the pages and staple them behind the cover. Have each child color a prepared booklet and a set of patterns. After reading each booklet page aloud, guide each youngster to glue the corresponding pattern where indicated. Then invite little ones to read their completed booklets along with you.

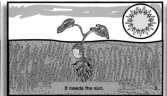
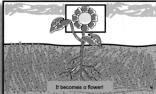

All in a Row

Your young florists create colorful flower arrangements at this center! Using one of the flower patterns on page 33, make a supply of construction paper flower cutouts in two different colors. Glue each flower to a craft stick stem. Press mounds of clay (or floral foam) along the bottom of a plastic flower box or other similar container. Place the flower box and flowers at a center. A center visitor stands the flowers in the box to make a pattern. For younger students, prepare paper strips with flower patterns for students to copy and extend.

Cultivate your growing learners with this
bouquet of ideas and reproducibles!

Placing Petals

Draw a simple flower without petals on a sheet of paper; then make a class supply. Also cut out a large supply of colorful construction paper petals that are sized to fit around the flower center. Give each child a flower and several petals.

To begin, say a pair of words. Have each youngster repeat them. If she hears the words rhyme, have her place a petal on her flower. Continue in the same manner until the flowers have a predetermined number of petals. Then invite little ones to glue on their petals.

Up Pops a Flower

Lead youngsters in this action song and watch your little sprouts grow!

(sung to the tune of "Pop! Goes the Weasel")

I plant a seed beneath the ground.	*Bend down and pretend to plant a seed.*
I give it a water shower.	*Pretend to water with a watering can.*
The sun shines down and what do you know?	*Hold hands in a circular shape above head.*
Up pops a flower!	*Squat down and pop up.*

SUNFLOWER
Daybreak

Musical Flowers

This circle-time game results in a vibrant basket of flowers! Use the patterns on page 33 to prepare a supply of flower cutouts in several different colors. Gather youngsters in a circle and place an empty basket or similar container in the center of the circle. Give every other child a flower.

To begin, play lively music as youngsters pass the flowers around the circle in the same direction. When you stop the music, direct each student holding a flower to silently identify its color. Announce a color. Have youngsters with a corresponding flower place their flowers in the basket and then return to the circle. Continue play in this manner, naming a different color each time, until all of the flowers are in the basket.

Flowery Snack

Color and cut out a copy of the recipe cards on page 34 and post them at your snack center. Arrange the ingredients and supplies for easy student access. Invite each youngster to follow the directions to make a flower snack.

Ingredients for one snack:
celery stick
large round cracker
5 small cheese-flavored square crackers

Supplies:
napkin for each child

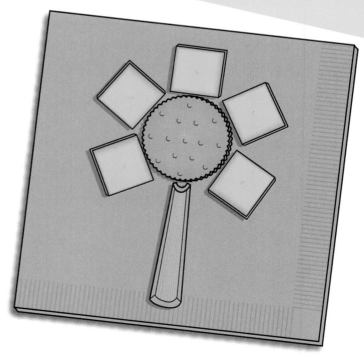

Blooming Bouquets

Make three construction paper copies of page 33, using a different color of paper for each copy. Cut out the flowers and tape a green pipe cleaner stem to each one. Place the flowers and three plastic vases in your small-group area.

To begin, invite a child to suggest one way to classify the flowers, such as by color or flower type. Then have youngsters work together to sort the flowers into the vases by the chosen method. Repeat the activity, inviting another child to suggest a different way to classify the flowers. If desired, place the materials at a center for independent practice.

Physical Health & Development

Gross-motor skills

Pollen Pass

Little ones act like busy bees during this class game! Use chalk to draw two large flowers at opposite ends of an open area. Place a class supply of large yellow pom-poms or beanbags (pollen) in the center of one flower. Line up students behind the flower with the pollen. Tell students that they are going to pretend to be buzzing bees carrying pollen from one flower to another. On your signal, the first bee picks up a piece of pollen, runs to the other flower, and places the pollen in its center. Each remaining bee takes a turn in the same manner until all of the pollen has been transferred.

Find a reproducible activity on page 35.

Growing a Flower

by _____

The seed is planted.

1

It needs water.   2

It needs the sun.   3

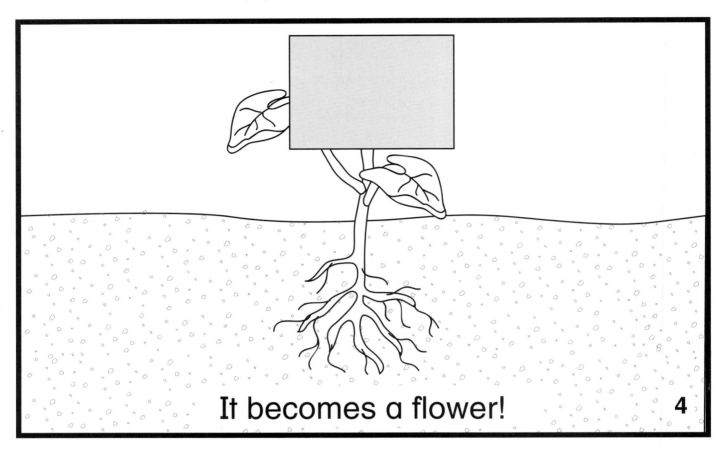

It becomes a flower!

4

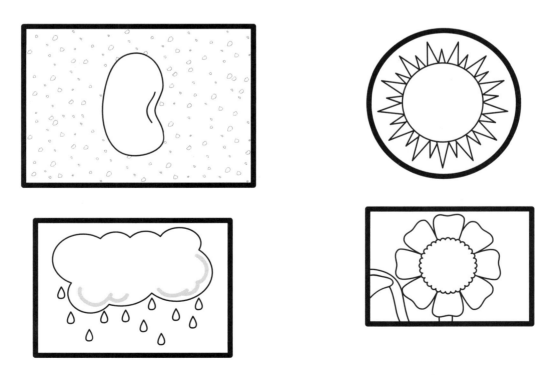

Use with "All in a Row" on page 26, "Musical Flowers" on page 28, "Blooming Bouquets" on page 29, and "Look How We Have Blossomed" on page 56.

TEC60973

TEC60973

TEC60973

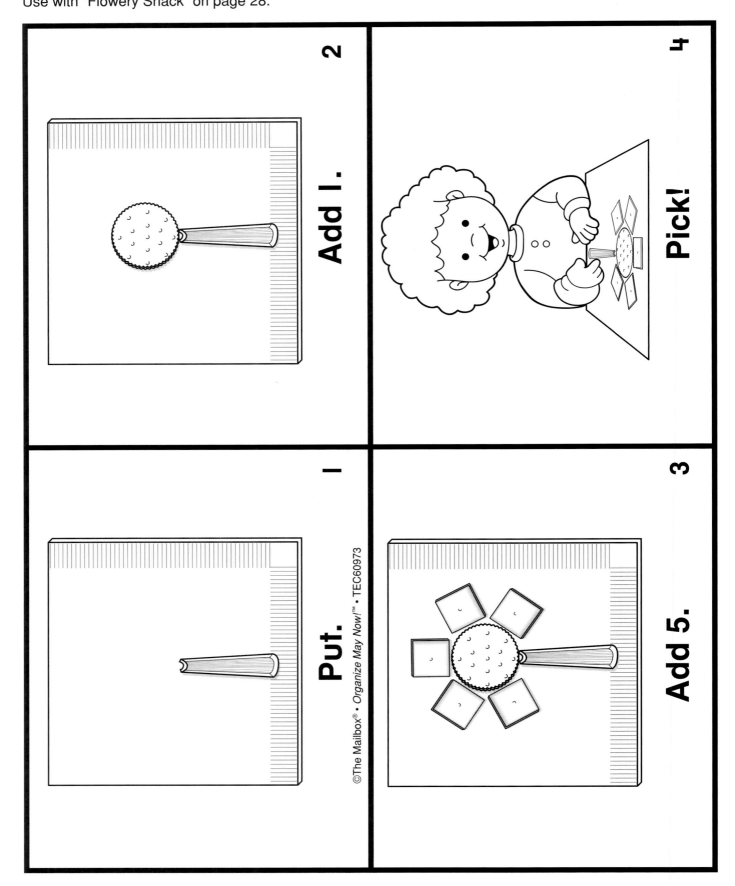

2

Add 1.

4

Pick!

1

Put.

©The Mailbox® • *Organize May Now!*™ • TEC60973

3

Add 5.

Dusty's Daisies

Name _____

🖍 Color the pictures that start like 🐨 .

Beginning Sound /d/   35

Butterflies

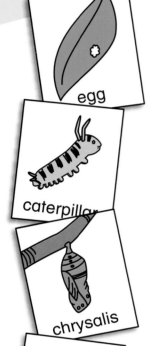

egg

caterpillar

chrysalis

butterfly

First Comes the Egg

How does a butterfly go from an egg to a beautiful insect? This simple action song will help you explain the life stages to your little ones! Color a copy of the cards on page 40 and place them in order in a pocket chart. Teach youngsters the song shown and then invite a volunteer to lead in singing as she points to each card in turn.

(sung to the tune of "Mary Wore Her Red Dress")

First comes the tiny egg, the tiny egg, the tiny egg. *Make tight fist.*
First comes the tiny egg; then…
Hatch! *Open hand wide.*

Here comes the caterpillar, caterpillar, caterpillar. *Extend and curl index finger.*
Here comes the caterpillar; then…
Yawn! *Yawn and stretch.*

Next comes the chrysalis, chrysalis, chrysalis. *Clasp hands together.*
Next comes the chrysalis; then…
Wow! *Slightly open hands.*

Out comes the butterfly, butterfly, butterfly. *Interlock thumbs and wiggle fingers in flying motion.*

Out comes the butterfly; fly…
Away!

Pretty Blue Butterfly

This small-group activity is just right for some word fun! Seat students in a circle and pass around a colored copy of the butterfly pattern on page 64. As each child holds the butterfly, invite him to supply a word to describe it. Write the word on a chart and then have him pass the butterfly to the next child. When the butterfly has made its way around the circle, review the many descriptive words.

This butterfly is…
pretty
blue
big

Flutter over for this collection of activities!

Here Comes a Butterfly

Have each child color a cutout of the butterfly pattern on page 68. Tape a craft stick to the back to make a puppet. Invite youngsters to move their butterfly puppets as indicated as you recite the rhyme. Keep the fun going by asking volunteers to substitute other positional phrases in the verse.

Here comes a butterfly,
Flying all around.
It flies [up high]
And then lands on the ground.

Substitute the underlined phrase with *down low, behind me, in front of me,* and *over me.*

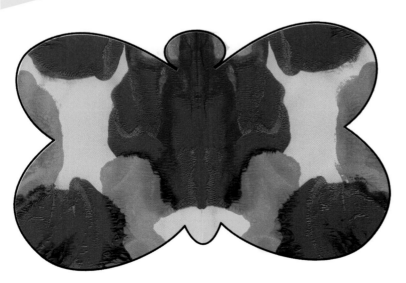

Painted Ladies

Share butterfly photos (or pictures from your favorite nonfiction book) and point out the many colors and designs found on butterfly wings. Then invite youngsters to make their own artistic butterflies with this easy painting technique! For each child, fold a sheet of construction paper in half. Help him open the paper and squirt two or three contrasting colors of paint into the fold. Next, have him refold the paper and rub the outside to blend and spread the paint. Then help him carefully unfold the paper. When the paint is dry, cut a large butterfly from each child's paper.

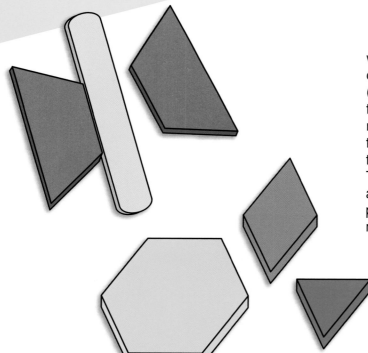

Take Wing!

Illustrate the similarities in a butterfly's wings with this partner activity. Give each twosome a craft stick (butterfly body) and jumbo pattern blocks (wings). Have one partner lay the craft stick on the floor and place a pattern block on one side to resemble a wing. Invite the other partner to copy the wing on the other side. Have the pair inspect the butterfly to make sure the wings look alike. Then invite the twosome to swap roles to make a different butterfly. If desired, encourage older preschoolers to use two blocks and then three (or more) to make each wing.

Beginning sounds

Sounds Like *Butterfly*

Mix copies of the picture cards on pages 41 and 42 and place them near the bottom of a pocket chart. Color and cut out a construction paper copy of the butterfly pattern on page 68; then tape a craft stick to the back to make a puppet. Holding the puppet, chant the rhyme shown. Next, ask a volunteer to hold the puppet and identify a card with a picture that begins with the /b/ sound like *butterfly*. Then have her move it to the top of the pocket chart. Continue in this manner until all the picture cards with the /b/ sound have been placed near the top of the chart.

This little butterfly flaps its wings,
Looking for a place to land.
It stops wherever it hears /b/;
Please give the butterfly a hand.

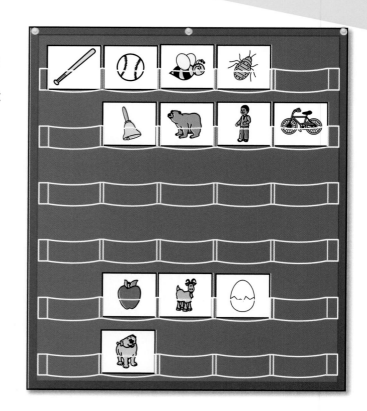

If I Were a Butterfly

This class-made book contains fanciful butterfly flight plans! Brainstorm with students a list of real and nonsense places a butterfly might fly. Next, give each child a copy of page 43 and write as she dictates to finish the sentence. Have her illustrate her page. Bind all the youngsters' pages between two covers and add a title. Then share the completed book, enlisting each student's help to read her page.

If I were a butterfly I'd fly to get ice cream.

Butterfly Garden

Butterflies flutter around the garden looking for tasty flower nectar in this musical activity! Tape a class supply of colorful construction paper flowers to the floor in an open area. Play soft music and invite youngsters to dance around the flowers like butterflies in a garden. Stop the music and announce, "Butterfly feeding time!" On this signal, each butterfly sits beside the nearest flower and pretends to drink its nectar. Then start the music again for another round of butterfly fluttering!

Find reproducible activities on pages 44–45.

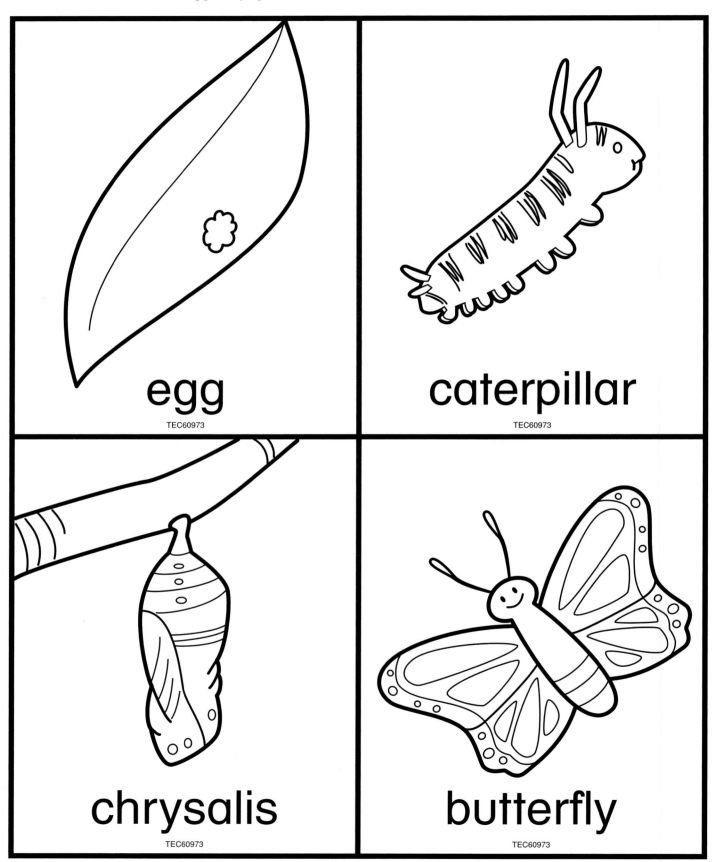

egg

TEC60973

caterpillar

TEC60973

chrysalis

TEC60973

butterfly

TEC60973

TEC60973

TEC60973

TEC60973

TEC60973

TEC60973

TEC60973

TEC60973

TEC60973

TEC60973

TEC60973

TEC60973

TEC60973

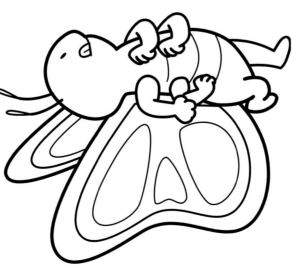

If I were a butterfly, I'd fly

Note to the teacher: Use with "If I Were a Butterfly" on page 39.

Bunches of Butterflies

Name _____

🖍 Color the big butterflies yellow.

🖍 Color the little butterflies blue.

Name _____

Flight of Fancy

✂ Cut.

Match the rhyming pictures.

Glue.

Mother's Day

Use these heartfelt ideas to help little ones honor their mothers or special loved ones on Mother's Day.

A Special Name

When youngsters participate in this class activity, "mom's" the word! On each of three large blank cards, write a different uppercase letter to spell *MOM*. While students are out of the room, hide the cards. To begin, explain to each student that even though her mom is not in the classroom, the word *mom* is. Then invite little ones to find the hidden letter cards. After the cards are found, help volunteers position the cards in a pocket chart to spell *MOM*. Next, have each child color and cut out a set of small letter cards (patterns on page 47). Help her put them in the correct order from left to right to spell *MOM*. Then have each youngster glue her sequenced cards to a sheet of paper and draw a picture of the loved one whom she calls Mom!

A Helping Pot

This student-made gift gives mothers the gift of helping. For each student, place a piece of clay or floral foam in a small foam cup (flowerpot). Copy the flower patterns on page 48 to make three flowers for each child. Also copy the label patterns on page 49 to make a class supply. Give each youngster three flower cutouts in a variety of colors and a label.

To make a helping pot, invite each student to think of three ways that he could help his mother. Write a different dictated response on each flower and then help him complete the label as indicated. Have each child glue his label to the flowerpot and glue the flowers to separate craft stick stems. Direct him to stand each flower in his flowerpot. Encourage each youngster to present his gift to its recipient on Mother's Day.

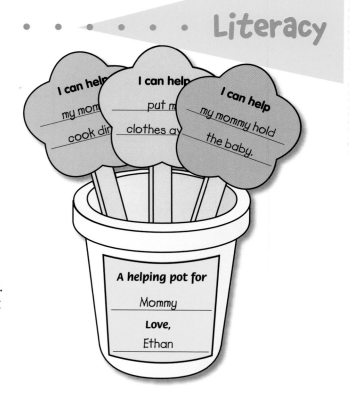

TEC60973

TEC60973

TEC60973

I can help

I can help

I can help

I can help

TEC60973

Use with "A Helping Pot" on page 46.

A helping pot for ____________________ **Love,** ____________________ ©The Mailbox® • *Organize May Now!*™ • TEC60973	**A helping pot for** ____________________ **Love,** ____________________ ©The Mailbox® • *Organize May Now!*™ • TEC60973
A helping pot for ____________________ **Love,** ____________________ ©The Mailbox® • *Organize May Now!*™ • TEC60973	**A helping pot for** ____________________ **Love,** ____________________ ©The Mailbox® • *Organize May Now!*™ • TEC60973
A helping pot for ____________________ **Love,** ____________________ ©The Mailbox® • *Organize May Now!*™ • TEC60973	**A helping pot for** ____________________ **Love,** ____________________ ©The Mailbox® • *Organize May Now!*™ • TEC60973

Arts & Crafts

Berry Basket

Welcome the very "berry" month of May with a strawberry basket! To make one, glue red tissue paper scraps along the outside of a plastic cup. While the glue is still wet, sprinkle glitter over the cup to resemble seeds. Glue green tissue paper scraps along the inside rim to resemble a strawberry cap. When the glue is dry, attach a green construction paper handle.

Ant Farm

All it takes is paper, fingerpaints, and imagination to make this cute project! To make an ant farm, spread brown fingerpaint all over a large sheet of fingerpaint paper. Then use one finger to draw an ant path and any other desired details in the paint. When the paint is dry, dip your pinkie into red paint and use it to make several ants along the path. Allow time for the paint to dry and then add details to the ants with a fine-tip black marker.

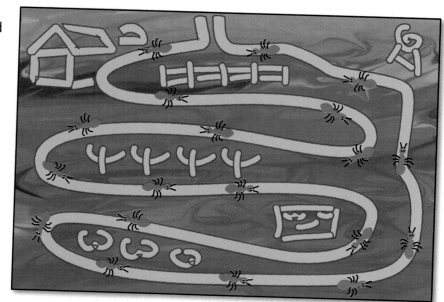

A "Berry" Special Mom

This Mother's Day card is "scent-sational"! In advance, mix white glue with strawberry-flavored drink mix until the desired color and scent is achieved. To make a card, dip the back of a plastic spoon in the glue mixture and press it on a sheet of construction paper to make a strawberry print. Make several strawberries in the same manner. After the glue is dry, attach a green star sticker to the top of each strawberry. Fold the paper in half to make a card. On the inside of the card, glue a copy of the poem from page 54 and sign your name.

Fireflies at Night

These cute fireflies zip around by the light of the moon! Glue a silver foil cupcake liner to a sheet of black construction paper to represent the moon. Using thick yellow paint, make several fingerprint fireflies on the paper. When the paint is dry, use yellow chalk to draw wings and antennae on the fireflies; then use a black marker to add facial features. If desired, add silver star stickers to complete the scene.

Create a Critter

The possibilities are endless when it comes to making this bug! Use the patterns on pages 54 and 55 to make two wings, a head, and six legs in a variety of colors for each child. Also, trim a 6" x 8" piece of colorful paper into an oval (bug body) for each student. Place each bug body part in a separate stack.

To make a bug, a child chooses a body, two wings, a head, and six legs. She glues the cutouts to the body as shown. When the glue is dry, she adds antennae and details with art materials, such as sticky dots, hole reinforcers, construction paper scraps, or markers.

Flower Garden

Spring is in full bloom with this painting technique! To make a flower stamper, snip one end of a drinking straw into evenly spaced sections. Spread out the resulting petals as shown. Prepare several stampers in this manner, varying the number and size of the petals. Dip the stamper into a shallow tray of paint and then press it on a sheet of construction paper to make a flower print. Make additional flowers using other stampers and different colors of paint. When the paint is dry, use markers to add a stem and leaves to each flower. If desired, use this technique on newsprint paper to make wrapping paper.

Sunny Sunflower

Here's a simple flower that is sure to brighten any day! To make a sunflower, glue a three-inch orange construction paper circle to a sheet of white construction paper. Make yellow fingerprints around the circle to resemble petals. Then add black pinkie prints to the circle to represent seeds. When the paint is dry, use markers to add a stem and leaves.

Striped Bee

To make a buzzing bee, squeeze dots of alternating yellow and black paint along the top of a white sheet of paper. Then use a ruler to pull the paint down the paper to resemble bee stripes. When the paint is dry, cut out a simple bee shape similar to the one shown. Use art materials to add details, and glue on wings cut from a transparency sheet.

Poem Pattern
Use with "A 'Berry' Special Mom" on page 51.

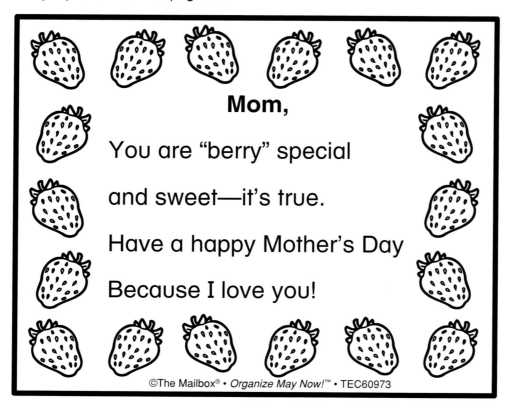

Mom,

You are "berry" special

and sweet—it's true.

Have a happy Mother's Day

Because I love you!

©The Mailbox® • *Organize May Now!*™ • TEC60973

Wing Pattern
Use with "Create a Critter" on page 52.

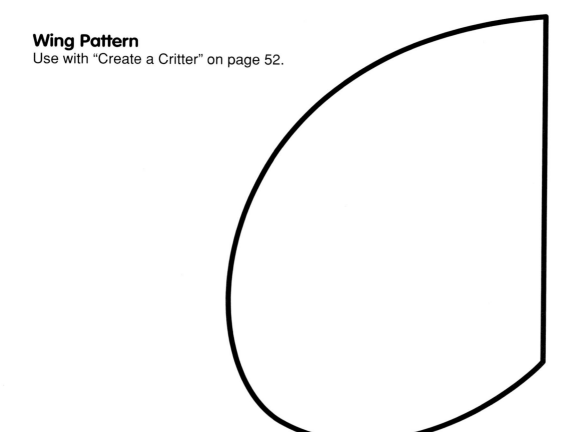

TEC60973

Look How We Have Blossomed!

Teena · Luis · Joey · Mary · Ava · Phil · Ian

Showcase your growing preschoolers with this seasonal bulletin board! Cut out a white construction paper flower for each student. (If desired, use the patterns on page 33.) Invite each child to color his flower and glue his photo to the flower. Display the flowers on a board with the title shown. Add a construction paper stem and personalized leaf to each flower. If desired, mount fringe-cut construction paper (grass) along the bottom of the board.

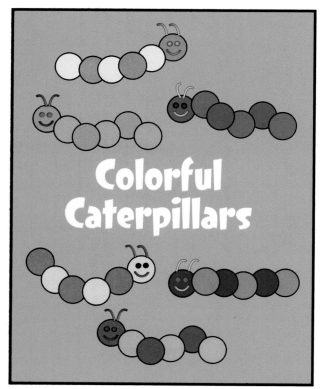

Colorful Caterpillars

Cut out a large supply of colorful construction paper circles. Give each child six circles in two different colors. Help her arrange the circles in an *AB* pattern. Then have her glue the circles together to resemble a caterpillar. Invite each youngster to add details using art materials. Display the caterpillars on a green background with the title shown.

Displays

Buzzing Bees

This interactive wall display is buzzing with math practice! Use the beehive pattern on page 58 to make five construction paper beehives. Label each hive with a different number from 1 to 5; then laminate them. Also copy, cut out, and laminate the bee cards on page 59; then store them in a resealable plastic bag. Display the hives on a wall within students' reach and place the bag nearby. Invite youngsters to use Sticky-Tac to mount the matching number of bees on each hive.

To prepare, draw a simple baseball cap at the top of a sheet of paper. Then make a copy for each student. Encourage each child to color the cap and incorporate it into a self-portrait. Display each child's completed picture along with a personalized baseball cutout (pattern on page 63) on a board similar to the one shown.

Beehive Pattern

Use with "Buzzing Bees" on page 57 and "Bee Buddies" on page 62.

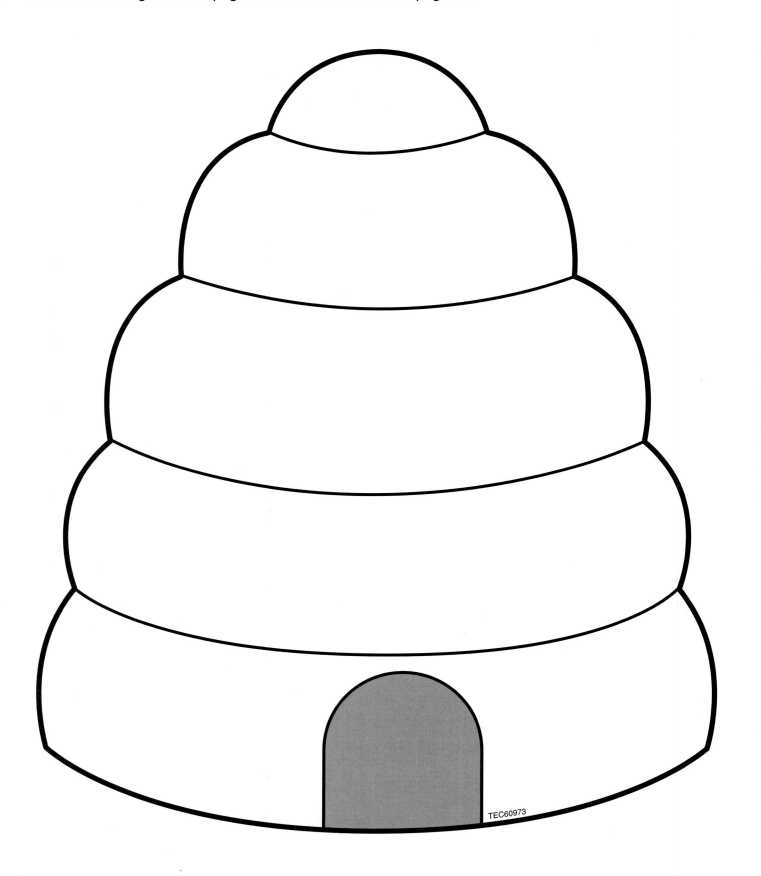

TEC60973

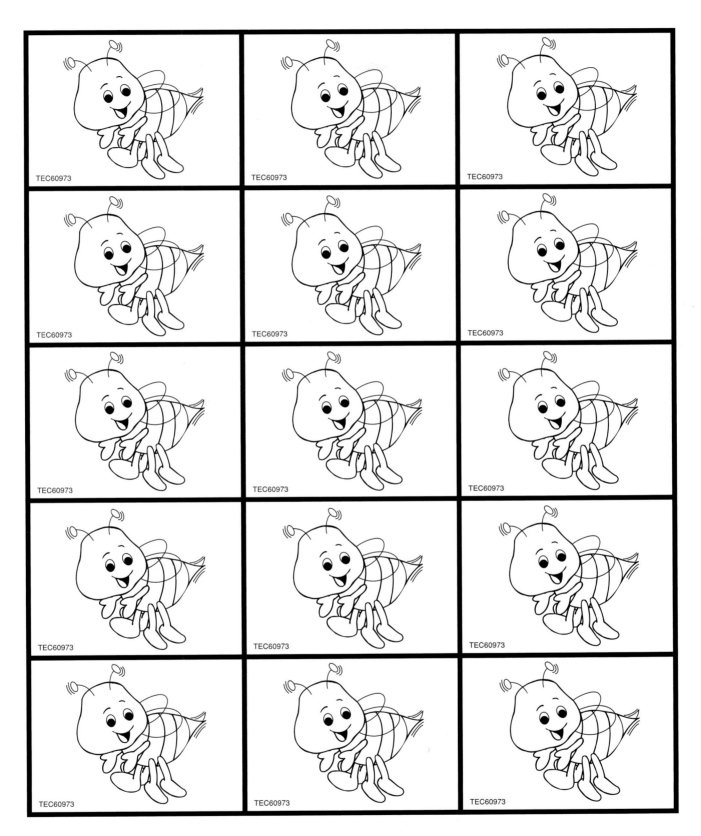

TEC60973

Centers

Literacy

Matching letters in own name

Play of the Day!

Spelling names with letter baseballs is sure to be a hit with your little ones! Cut out a supply of construction paper baseballs (pattern on page 63) and program each with a different uppercase or lowercase letter needed to spell each child's name. (Make sure to account for names in which the same lowercase letters appear more than once.) Store the prepared baseballs in a catcher's mitt or a baseball cap along with student name cards. To play, a child uses his name card as a guide to find and then match the letters in his name. For extra practice, have youngsters use the name cards and balls to spell their classmates' names.

Physical Health & Development

Fine-motor skills

Butterfly Beauties

Celebrate spring with these beautiful butterflies! Cut out several copies of the butterfly pattern on page 64 and laminate them. Place the butterflies and several colors of play dough at a center. A child rolls, twists, and molds the play dough to make decorations for a butterfly's wings. Encourage older preschoolers to make the same designs on each wing so the wings are symmetrical.

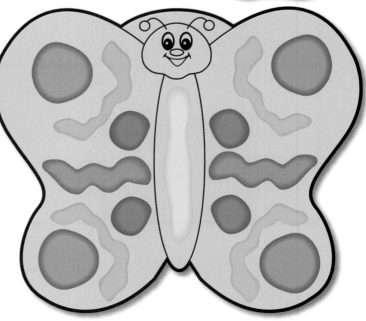

Matching sets

Lovely Ladybugs

These little ladybugs call for youngsters to match their spots! Make six simple ladybugs similar to the ones shown. Program each of the ladybugs with a number from 0 to 5 and draw a corresponding number of spots on each. Place the bugs and a container holding 15 black pom-poms at a center. A child chooses a ladybug and places a pom-pom on each spot. He continues in this manner for each remaining bug. For a challenge, have him identify the numeral and then count the spots.

Math

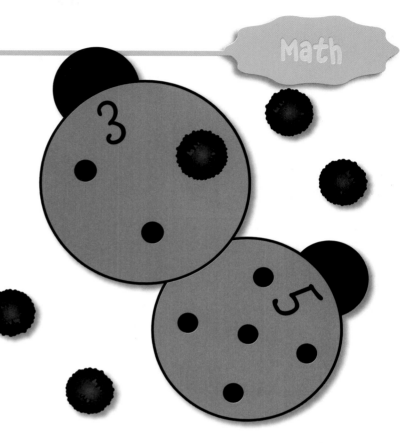

Creative Arts

Dramatic play

Growing a Garden

Youngsters put their green thumbs to work in this garden experience! Partially fill your sensory tub with new potting soil. Place children's hand-held gardening tools and gloves, artificial flowers, and an empty watering can in a container beside the tub. If desired, add artificial fishing worms to the soil. A visiting gardener slips on the gloves and uses the tools to create a well-tended garden with beautiful flowers.

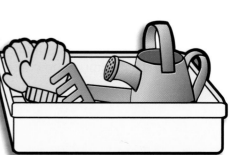

Visual discrimination

Bee Buddies

Partners make a beeline to match these bees! Cut out two yellow construction paper copies of the bee cards on page 65. Glue one set of cards to a large paper beehive (pattern on page 58). Place the hive and the other set of bee cards at a center. A child takes a card, looks for its match on the hive, and places the card on its twin. Her partner takes a turn in a similar manner. Play continues until all the bees on the hive have a match. When they do, the twosome collects the cards and plays again.

Matching numbers

Math

Berry Pickin'

Little ones take a trip to the strawberry patch without even leaving the classroom! To create the patch, place shredded green paper and leaf cutouts in your sensory tub to represent strawberry plants. Then cut out several construction paper copies of the strawberry patterns on page 63. Program each berry with a number from 0 to 5 and add them to the patch. Also label baskets to match the numbers on the berries and set them next to the patch. A child picks a berry from the patch, identifies the number, and places the berry in the matching basket. She continues with the remaining berries in the same manner. For older berry pickers, program the strawberries with seeds and have students count the seeds, identify the number, and place the berry in the matching basket.

TEC60973

Strawberry Patterns
Use with "Fresh-Picked Practice" on page 21 and "Berry Pickin'" on page 62.

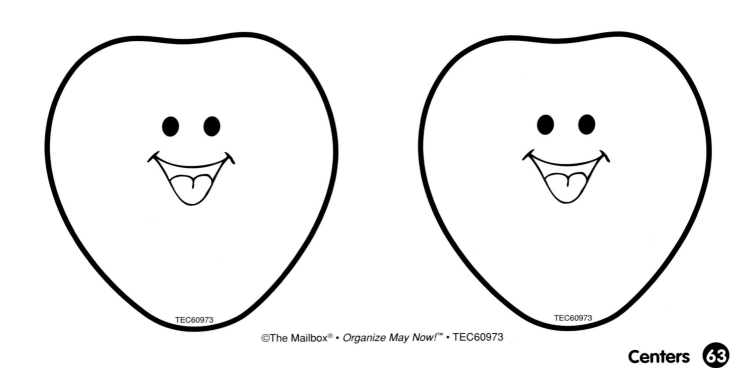

TEC60973   TEC60973

Butterfly Pattern

Use with "Pretty Blue Butterfly" on page 36 and "Butterfly Beauties" on page 60.

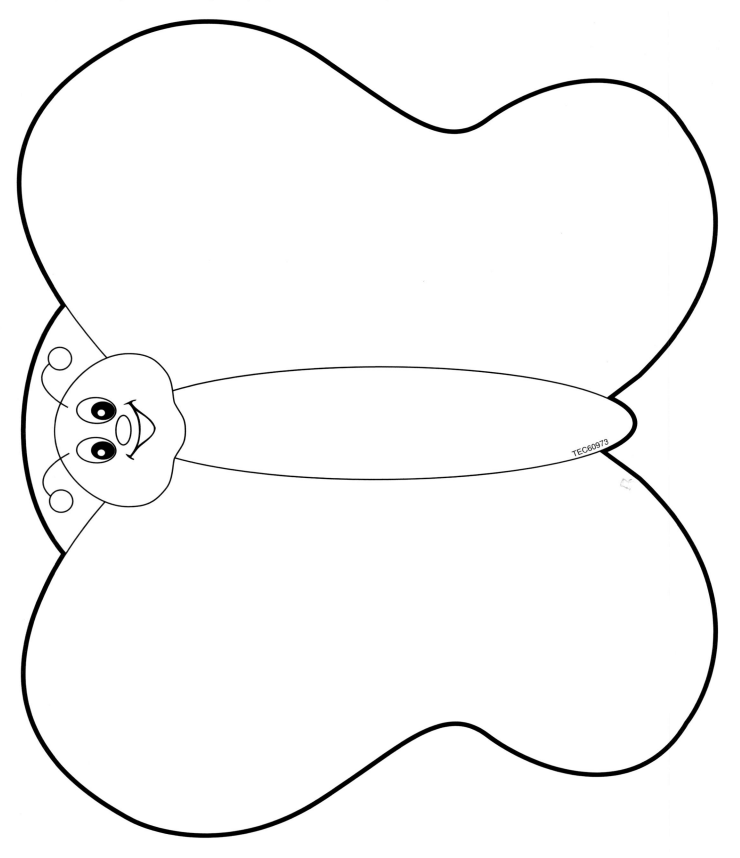

TEC60973

Centers 65

Literacy

Matching letters

Fluttering to Flowers

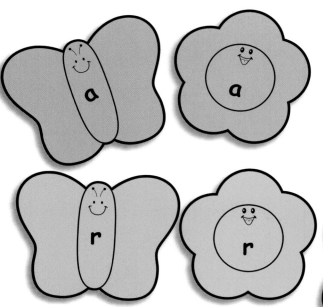

To prepare, copy and cut out a butterfly and a flower pattern (page 68) for every two students. Label each pattern pair with matching letters. Then give each youngster a butterfly or flower cutout. Direct the students with the flowers to spread out in an open area and hold their flowers face out. On your signal, invite each butterfly to fly around, search for its matching flower, and stand beside it. When all pairs are matched, redistribute the cutouts for another round of play. For an added challenge, label the cutouts for uppercase and lowercase letter matching.

Reasoning ═══════════════ **Approaches to Learning**

Going Buggy!

Who's that bug in the rug? It's one of your preschoolers, of course! Gather youngsters in a circle. Ask one child to be the guesser and have him leave the circle and cover his eyes. Then silently choose another student to be the bug. Have the bug hide underneath a towel in the center of the circle. Invite the guesser back to the circle and then lead youngsters in the chant shown. Give the guesser three chances to guess who the bug in the rug is. (Provide clues as needed.) Once the bug is identified, he becomes the guesser for the next round of play. Continue in this manner until each child has had a turn to be the bug.

Bug in the rug,
Bug in the rug,
Just who is that
Bug in the rug?

Physical Health & Development

Seed, Seed, Sprout

Please your little sprouts with this game! In a large open area, seat youngsters in a circle. Assign one child to be the gardener and give her an empty plastic watering can to hold. To play, the gardener walks around the circle gently tapping each classmate's shoulder with her hand while saying the word *seed.* Then the gardener pretends to water a student's head while saying the word *sprout.* The chosen student acts like a sprouting seed by slowly standing up. Then the two students switch places and the sprout becomes the gardener for another round of play.

Language Development

Following directions

Fruit Salad

Juicy fruits are the perfect treat for a warm spring day, so why not invite little ones to make a life-size fruit salad? To prepare, copy and cut out the fruit cards on page 69 so that there is one for each child. Have each child identify and color the fruit on his card. To begin, have youngsters sit in a circle with their cards. Announce one or more fruits. Invite all students with the corresponding cards to come to the center of the circle to make a fruit salad. After scanning for accuracy, have youngsters return to the circle. Then announce a different combination of fruits for the next silly salad!

Butterfly Pattern

Use with "Here Comes a Butterfly" on page 37, "Sounds Like *Butterfly*" on page 38, "Fluttering to Flowers" on page 66 and "Butterfly Bunches" on page 70.

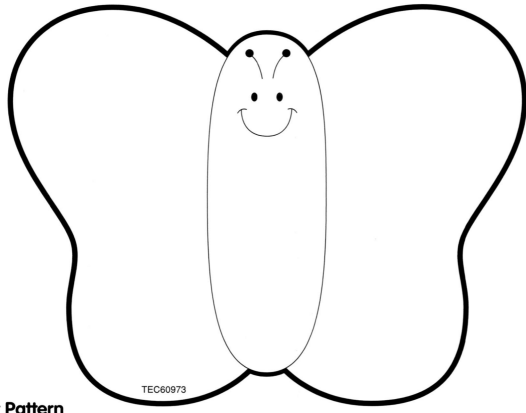

TEC60973

Flower Pattern

Use with "Fluttering to Flowers" on page 66.

TEC60973

TEC60973

TEC60973

TEC60973

TEC60973

Management Tips

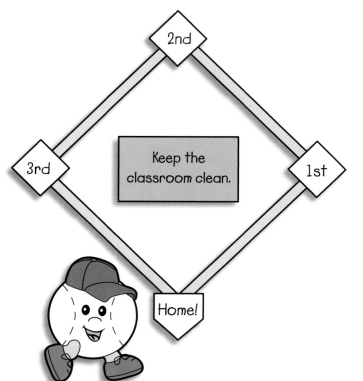

2nd

3rd

Keep the classroom clean.

1st

Home!

Major-League Motivator

Step out of the dugout and pitch this positive behavior incentive to your young sluggers. Display a baseball diamond in an easily accessible location. In the middle of the diamond, post a goal that you would like the class to work on, such as sharing toys or walking quietly in the hall. Color and cut out a copy of the baseball buddy on page 71, and place him next to home plate. Each time the class achieves its goal, invite a youngster to move the buddy to the next base. When a run is scored, reward the class with a treat or special privilege. When students are ready for a new challenge, simply post a new goal and return the baseball buddy to the batter's box.

Butterfly Bunches

Here's a colorful tip to help sort students into small groups. Use the butterfly pattern on page 68 to make a class supply of construction paper butterflies in different colors. (The number of colors will depend on the number of groups.) To create student groups, randomly distribute the butterflies to your youngsters and ask students to group themselves by color. As youngsters work, use the color codes to acknowledge the groups that are working well together.

TEC60973

Songs, Poems, &

Fluttering Butterflies

Little ones will flutter through this happy tune!

(sung to the tune of "Twinkle, Twinkle, Little Star")

Butterflies fly all around,
Fluttering without a sound.
Their small wings are colored bright,
Flashing in the warm sunlight.
Butterflies fly through the air,
In the garden—everywhere!

"Strawberry-licious"!
Strawberries are always in season with this sweet fingerplay.

Strawberries, strawberries everywhere.
I see some ripe, red berries to share.
I'll pick some sweet, juicy ones for you.
Then let's fill a basket with them too.

I like strawberry jam on my toast,
But fresh from the garden is what I like most!

Point to ground.
Hold hands out with palms up.
Point to a neighbor.
*Bend down and pretend to pick
   strawberries.*
Rub tummy and say, "Yum!"
Smile and hug yourself.

Fingerplays

Flowers

Everyone will be in the mood to pick posies after reciting this flowery poem.

Flowers are many sizes
And many colors, too:
Bright yellow daffodils,
Pansies of white and blue.

Flowers grow in a garden
Or under leafy trees.
They sway so beautifully,
Like dancers in the breeze.

Cinco de Mayo!

Celebrate the fifth of May with this party song.

(sung to the tune of "Pop! Goes the Weasel")

It is time to celebrate
With family and friends.
Piñatas swinging overhead—
Cinco de Mayo!

Today is the fifth of May,
Parades, dancing, and music.
That's the way the party goes—
Cinco de Mayo!

Flower Power

Two ready-to-use center mats and cards

Extending patterns

Materials:
center mat sections to the right and on page 77
center cards on page 79
2 resealable plastic bags

Preparing the center:
Cut out the center mat sections on each page and glue them together where indicated to make two separate mats. Cut out the cards and place each set in a separate bag. Store each set of cards with its matching mat.

Using the center:
1. A child removes the cards from a bag and lays them faceup in the center area.
2. She reads the pattern on the mat, naming the colors of the flowers from left to right as she points to each one.
3. She extends the pattern by placing the cards on the mat.
4. To verify her work, she reads the pattern from beginning to end as she points to each flower.
5. She repeats Steps 1–4 for the other mat and set of cards.

Family Follow-Up
After a youngster completes the center, have her take home a copy of page 81 to complete with a parent.

Glue here.

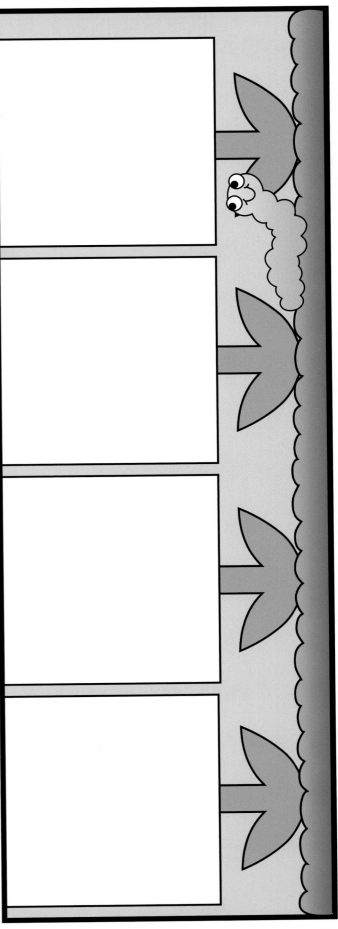

©The Mailbox® • *Organize May Now!*™ • TEC60973

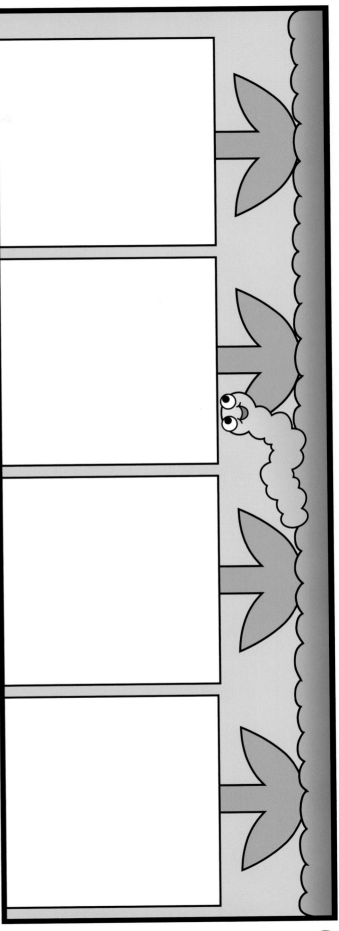

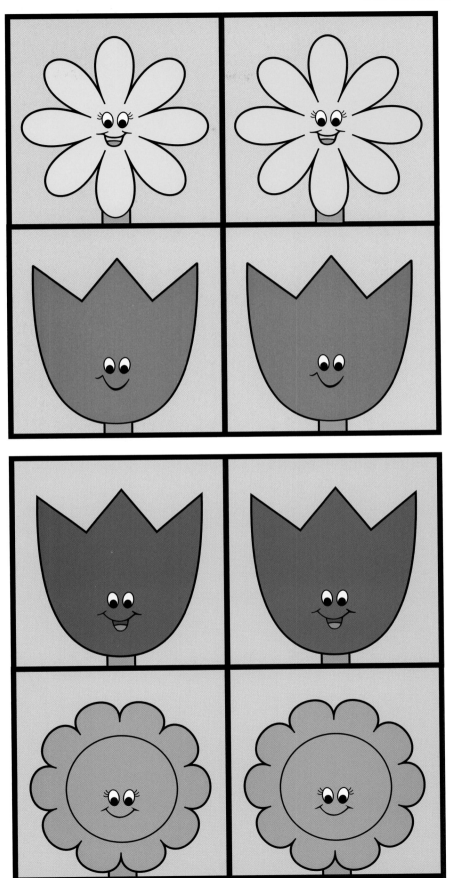

Flower Power
TEC60973

Flower Power
TEC60973

Flower Power
TEC60973

Flower Power
TEC60973

Flower Power
TEC60973

Flower Power
TEC60973

Flower Power
TEC60973

Flower Power
TEC60973

Dear Parent,
We have been making simple patterns. For each row of flowers below, have your child choose two colors of crayons. Then help your youngster color the flowers in each row, alternating colors to make two simple patterns.

Busy Bees

A ready-to-use center mat and cards

Materials:

center mat to the right
center cards on pages 85 and 87
resealable plastic bag

Preparing the center:

Cut out the cards and put them in the bag.

Using the center:

1. A child removes the cards from the bag and lays them letter side up in the center area.
2. He chooses an uppercase letter and then finds the matching lowercase letter.
3. He flips the cards over. If the backs of the cards have matching pictures, he places the cards on the mat. If the pictures do not match, he finds the correct lowercase letter card; then he places the cards on the mat.
4. He repeats Steps 2 and 3 until all the cards are placed on the mat.

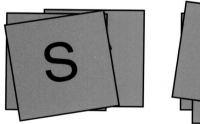

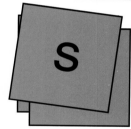

Family Follow-Up

After a youngster completes the center, have him take home a copy of page 89 to complete with a parent.

Busy Bees

Match.
Check.
Put.

M   m

C   c

T   t

Busy Bees
TEC60973

Busy Bees
TEC60973

Busy Bees
TEC60973

Busy Bees
TEC60973

Busy Bees
TEC60973

Busy Bees
TEC60973

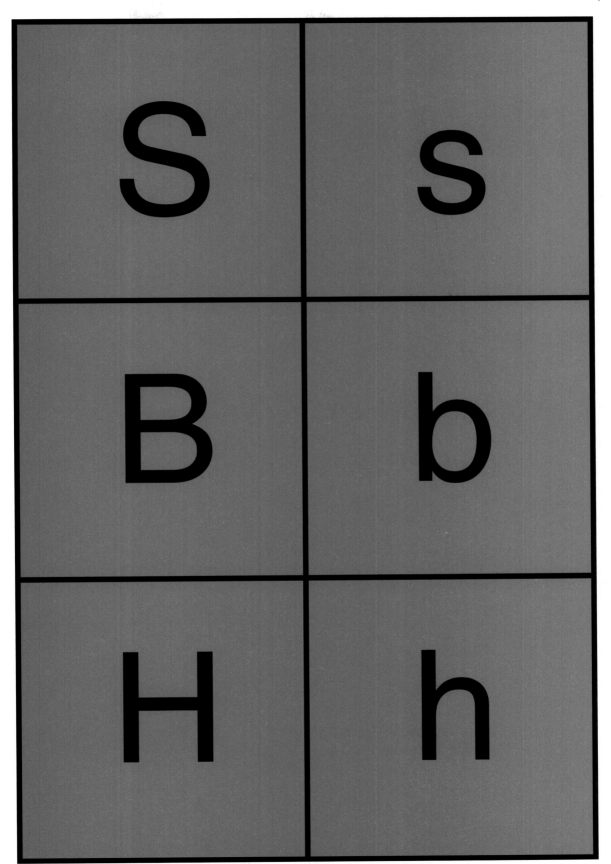

Busy Bees
TEC60973

Busy Bees
TEC60973

Busy Bees
TEC60973

Busy Bees
TEC60973

Busy Bees
TEC60973

Busy Bees
TEC60973

Dear Parent,

We have been matching uppercase and lowercase letters. Help your child draw a line from each uppercase letter on the left side of the paper to the corresponding lowercase letter on the right side of the paper.

B

M

H

T

h

t

b

m

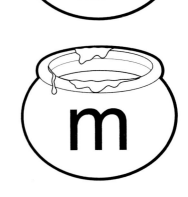

So Hungry!

Name _____

Trace.

Tracing

Name _____

Trace.

Home,
Sweet
Home

In Full Bloom

Name _____

Trace.

Color.

Beautiful Butterfly

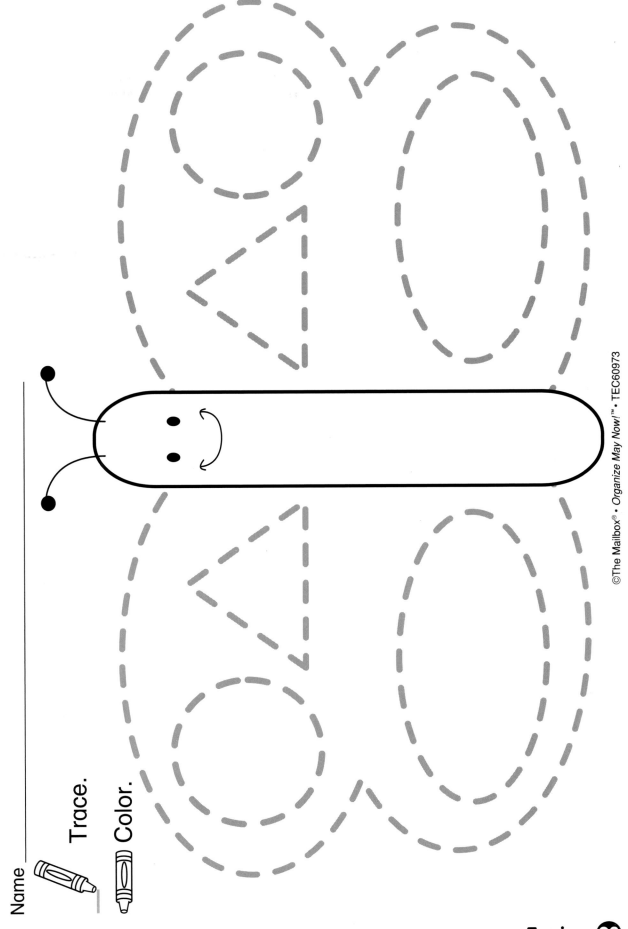

Name _____

🖍 Trace.

🖍 Color.

Mother's Day!

Name _____

 Color.

 Cut.

 Glue.

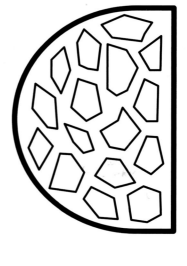

Happy Mother's Day

Cut and Glue

Supersize Strawberries

Name _____

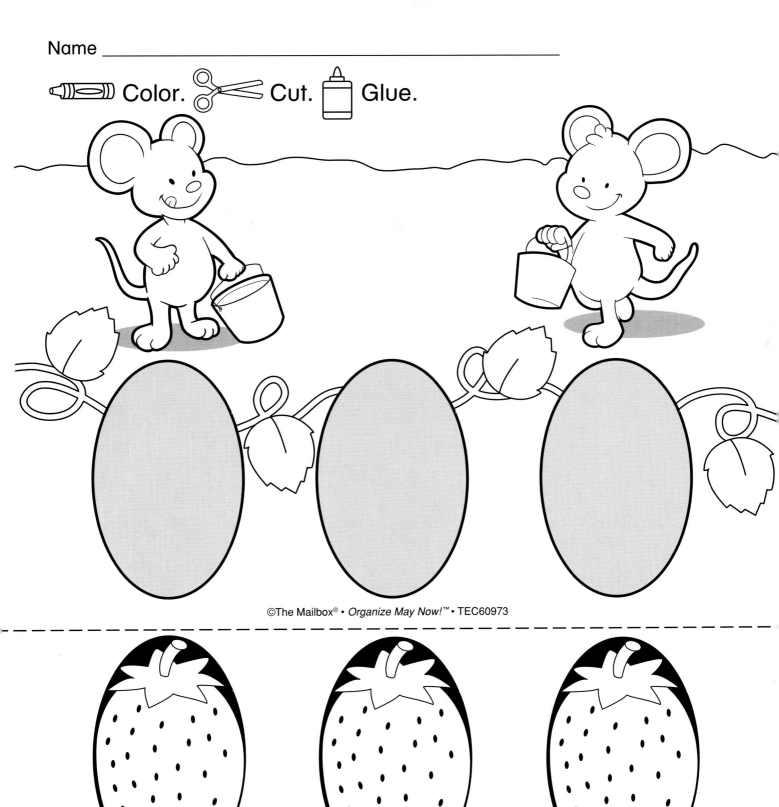

Color. Cut. Glue.

Leapfrog

Name _____

Color.

Cut.

Glue.

Cut and Glue